Scarves & How to Wear Them

By Kathleen Lukens

All scarves in this book are hand dyed silk and rayon scarves from Hana Lima Hand Dyes.

The author can be reached at:
http://hanalimahanddyes.blogspot.com or
klukens@prodigy.net

Scarves & How to Wear Them - Through the Loop

1. Fold your scarf in half lengthwise and drape around your neck with the fold on one side of the front and the loose ends on the other side.

2. Slip the loose ends through the folded end.

Scarves & How to Wear Them - Through the Loop

3. Pull on the loose ends to adjust.

Scarves & How to Wear Them - Through the Loop Twice

1. Fold your scarf in half lengthwise and drape it around your neck with the fold on one side of the front and the loose ends on the other side.

2. Take ONE of the long ends and pull it through the loop.

Scarves & How to Wear Them - Through the Loop Twice

3. Then take the other long end, lay it under the loop and pull it through.

4. Adjust to the length you want.

Scarves & How to Wear Them - Over the Shoulder #1

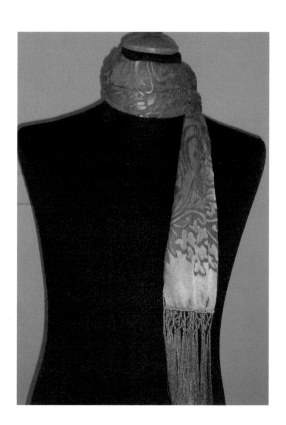

1. Drape the scarf around your neck, starting in the front this time, with one end longer than the other. The ends will be in the back. Then bring the ends around to the front.

2. Take the longer end and toss it over your shoulder.

Scarves & How to Wear Them - Over the Shoulder #2

1. Place the scarf around your neck with one end longer than the other.

2. Toss the longer end over your shoulder and arrange the scarf loosely at your neck.

Scarves & How to Wear Them - The Cowl

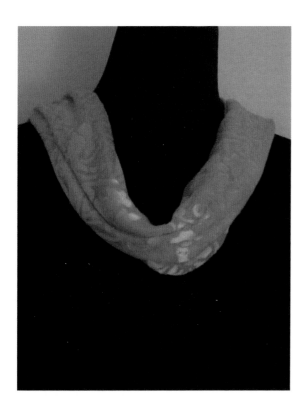

1. Drape your scarf around your neck, leaving it loose in the front.

2. Take the ends and wrap then around to the front   Adjust the neckline if necessary.

Scarves & How to Wear Them - A Simple Knot

1. Place the scarf around your neck with the ends hanging evenly in the front. This is good if you're petite and want to add the illusion of height. And it works for oblong scarves of any length.

 2. You could either leave the ends dangling as in step 1. Or you can take the two ends and tie them in a knot, shown above.

Scarves & How to Wear Them - The V-Neck Look

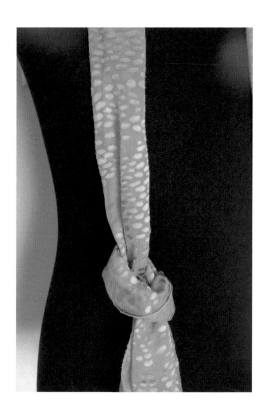

1. Wrap an oblong scarf around your neck leaving one end longer than the other.

2. Tie a loose knot in the longer end.

Scarves & How to Wear Them - The V-Neck Look

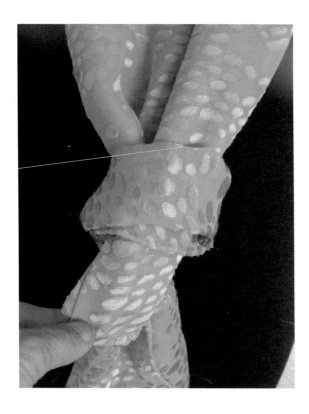

3. Pull the shorter end through the knot.

4. Pull on the ends to adjust.

Scarves & How to Wear Them - Interlocking Chains

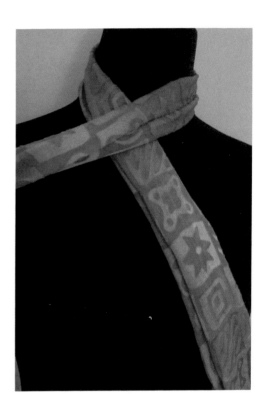

1. Place the scarf around your neck with the ends even.

2. Cross the ends once.

Scarves & How to Wear Them - Interlocking Chains

3. Cross the ends again.

4. Tie in the back.

Scarves & How to Wear Them - The Puff

1. Place the scarf around your neck with one end longer than the other

2. Tie the ends in a square knot.

Scarves & How to Wear Them - The Puff

3. Feed some of the longer end behind the knot to form a "puff"

4. Let the puff sit over the knot.

Scarves & How to Wear Them - The Half Bow

1. Put the scarf around your neck with one end longer than the other end.

2. Cross the longer end over the shorter end.

Scarves & How to Wear Them - The Half Bow

3. Pull the longer end up behind the loop at the neck and at the same time, pull on the shorter end to tighten

4. Adjust as needed. This is best for narrow scarves. If you want to use a wider scarf, fold it in half to make it narrow. It will work fine but will be bulkier.

Scarves & How to Wear Them - The Hidden Knot

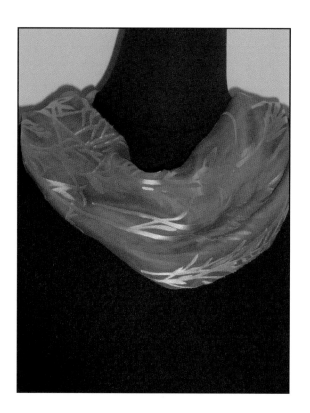

1. Fold a wide and long oblong scarf in half and wrap it around your neck with the ends in the back.

2. Cross the ends in the back and bring them around to the front.

Scarves & How to Wear Them - The Hidden Knot

3. Tie the ends in a knot close to your neck.

4. Tuck the knot under the layer at your neck.

Scarves & How to Wear Them - The Circle

1. Place the scarf over your head with the seam or knot in the back. If you don't have a circle or tube scarf, you can tie the ends of an oblong scarf in a small knot.

2. Depending on the length of your scarf, you could wear it as is or go one step further by twisting the right side over the left side to form another loop and putting the loop over your head.

Scarves & How to Wear Them - The Circle

3. You can either wear it as is, or go on to step 4 for one more wrap.

4. If your scarf is long enough and you want your scarf closer to the neck, make one more twist and put that over your head. It should now fit close to the neck.

Scarves & How to Wear Them - The Sailor Collar

1. Fold a wide, oblong scarf in half. Hold the opposite diagonal ends of the scarf and lift. It will fall naturally into two triangles.

2. Place the scarf around your neck with the ends in the front (the fold will be in the back).

Scarves & How to Wear Them - The Sailor Collar

3. Tie the ends in a knot.

4. You can also wear the knot in the back or to the side for two different looks.

Scarves & How to Wear Them - Loop and Twist

1. Fold your scarf in half and wrap it around your neck with the ends about the same length in front.

2. Put the ends through the loop.

Scarves & How to Wear Them - Loop and Twist

3. Twist the remaining loop and put the ends through again.

4. Adjust to the length you prefer.

Scarves & How to Wear Them - Thru the Loop Twice

1. Place your oblong scarf so it loosely covers the front of your neck and the ends hang down in the back. Then bring the ends around to the front.

2. Put one end through the loop at your neck. Do this again with the same end so it has been through the loop twice.

Scarves & How to Wear Them - Thru the Loop Twice

3. Repeat with the other end, putting it through the same neck loop twice.

4. Adjust to the length you prefer. Note: if you put the ends through the loop from the bottom instead of putting them over the top, you get still another look.

Scarves & How to Wear Them - The Chain

1. Drape your oblong scarf around your neck with the ends hanging evenly in the front.

2. Cross one end over the other.

Scarves & How to Wear Them - The Chain

3. Repeat until the chain is as long as you want it.

4. Knot the ends at the bottom of the chain.

Scarves & How to Wear Them - Spiral Through the Loop

1. Twist two coordinating scarves into a spiral.

2. Put the scarves around your neck loosely and bring the ends to the front.

Scarves & How to Wear Them - Spiral Thru the Loop

3. Pull one end through the loop. Then repeat with the other end.

4. Adjust to the length you prefer.

Scarves & How to Wear Them - The Halter #1

1. Place one oblong scarf around your bust and tie in a knot.

2. Loop another scarf through the first one in the front and tie in a knot at the back of your neck.

Scarves & How to Wear Them - The Halter #2

1. Fold your large oblong or square shawl into a triangle. With the points at the top, cross the two ends and tie securely at the back of your neck.

2. Tie the other two ends into a knot at the back of your waist.

Scarves & How to Wear Them - Mini & Maxi Skirts

1. For the maxi skirt, fold your large oblong scarf in half so the length is longer than the width. Put the scarf behind you and wrap to the front. Tie the ends securely in a knot at the waist or hips on the side or in front.

2. For the mini skirt look, fold your shawl in half so that the length is shorter than the width. Then wrap and tie as shown in Step 1.

Scarves & How to Wear Them - The Pareo

1. All of these pareos start by wrapping the scarf from back to front.

For this version, tie the ends securely in the front above your bust.

2. An alternate version is to tie the ends on your shoulder. Put one end under your arm and the other end over your shoulder. Tie the ends securely on your shoulder.

Scarves & How to Wear Them - The Pareo

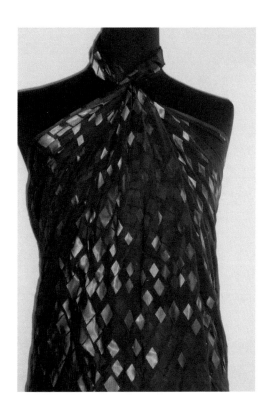 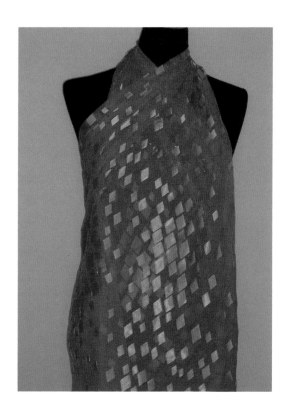

1. In this version, you take both ends and twist them together. Then tie them at the back of your neck.

2. And in this version, you cross both ends in the front and tie them around your neck in the back.

Scarves & How to Wear Them

No matter how many scarves you have, it's never enough! Scarves are a great way to update your wardrobe without breaking the bank. What other accessory can change your daytime outfit into fashionable evening wear with so little effort? The ideas in this book are just the tip of the iceberg when it comes to wearing scarves. You can also tie your scarf around your head, around your waist as a belt, and on the handle of your purse. The possibilities are endless!

Made in the USA
Charleston, SC
25 August 2013